GW01396008

Maths Activity Book

for ages 3-4

This CGP book is bursting with bright and colourful Maths activities for pre-school children.

It's a brilliant way to introduce the essential topics — and it's stacks of fun too!

Helpful Hints

- A grown-up can help you read the questions.
  Let them know which activities you enjoy the most.

- Find a nice place to work. Make sure
  you're comfortable at your desk or table.

- Use a pencil to write or draw your answers.
  You can use coloured pencils to colour in the pictures.

- Work neatly, and try to keep your pencil inside the lines.

- Writing the numbers nice and clearly is really important —
  you can practise this on a separate piece of paper.

- The 'Counting Cards' activity in the centre uses maths skills
  from the whole book — you may want to save this until last.

Published by CGP

ISBN: 978 1 78908 605 8

Editors: Adam Bartlett, Michael Bushell, Ben Train

With thanks to Ruth Greenhalgh, Joanne Haslett and Gail Renaud for the proofreading.

With thanks to Jan Greenway for the copyright research.

Printed by Elanders Ltd, Newcastle upon Tyne.
Cover and graphics used throughout the book © www.edu-clips.com
Cover design concept by emc design ltd.

Text, design, layout and original illustrations
© Coordination Group Publications Ltd. (CGP) 2020
All rights reserved.

Photocopying this book is not permitted, even if you have a CLA licence.
Extra copies are available from CGP with next day delivery • 0800 1712 712 • www.cgpbooks.co.uk

Contents

The Number 1

How It Works

This is 1 plane.

This is 1 bag.

Now Try These

Trace the number 1 with your finger.
Then join the dots to write it.

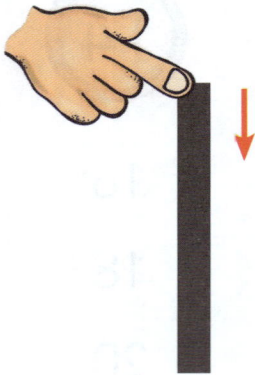

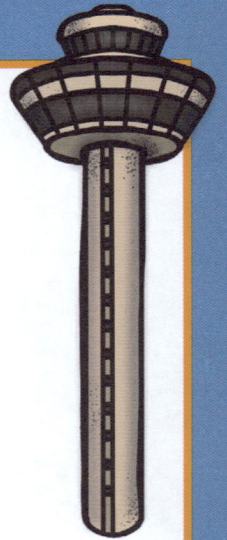

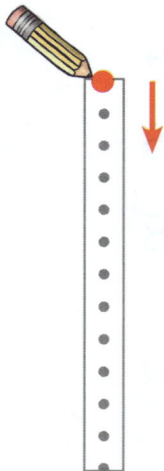

Colour in 1 ticket.

Colour in 1 suitcase.

Match the word to the picture.

1 desk

1 plane

1 book

Write in the 1s to finish the picture.

If you're flying high with number 1, colour in the smiley face!

3

The Number 2

How It Works

Count to 2.

1

2

There are 2 pears.

Now Try These

Trace the number 2 with your finger.
Then join the dots to write it.

Circle the tree that has 2 apples.

Count up from 1 to 2 strawberries. Colour them in.

Draw lines to match 2 pieces of each fruit.

Colour all the shapes with
the number 2 in them.
What can you see?

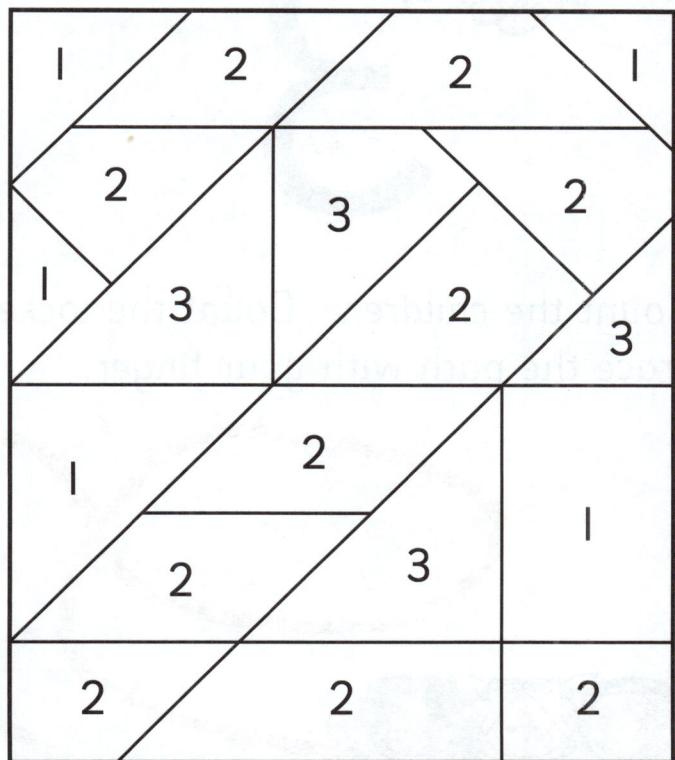

1	2	2	1
2		3	2
1	3	2	3
1		2	
	2	3	1
2		2	2

Colour in the smiley face — your number skills are growing fast!

5

The Number 3

How It Works

Count to 3.

1   **2**   **3**

There are 3 balls.

Now Try These

Trace the number 3 with your finger.
Then join the dots to write it.

  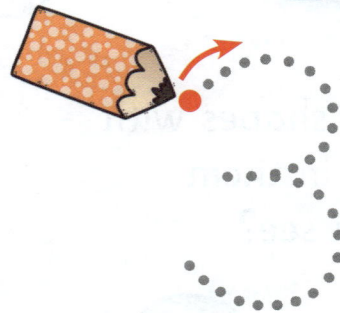

Count the children. Count the lockers.
Trace the path with your finger.

Circle the odd one out.

Find and circle all of the groups of 3 in the picture below.

You know the number 3 — well done! Colour in the smiley face.

The Number 4

How It Works

Count to 4.

1   2   3   4

There are 4 bird houses.

Now Try These

Trace the number 4 with your finger.
Then join the dots to write it.

Colour in 4 birds.

Write the number 4.

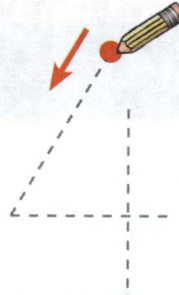

Count the number of deer hiding in the forest.

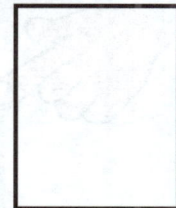

deer

Draw 4 eggs in the nest below.

How It Works

Count to 5.

1
2
3
4
5

There are 5 bats.

Now Try These

Trace the number 5 with your finger.
Then join the dots to write it.

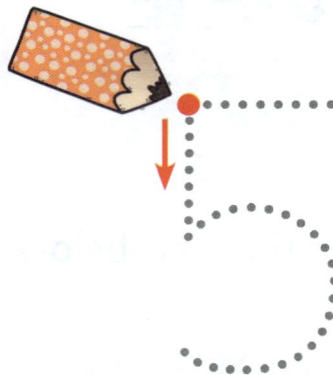

5

Ssshhhhh. How many children are sleeping?
Write the number in the box.

Count the groups and circle the odd one out.

Trace the way back to room number 5.

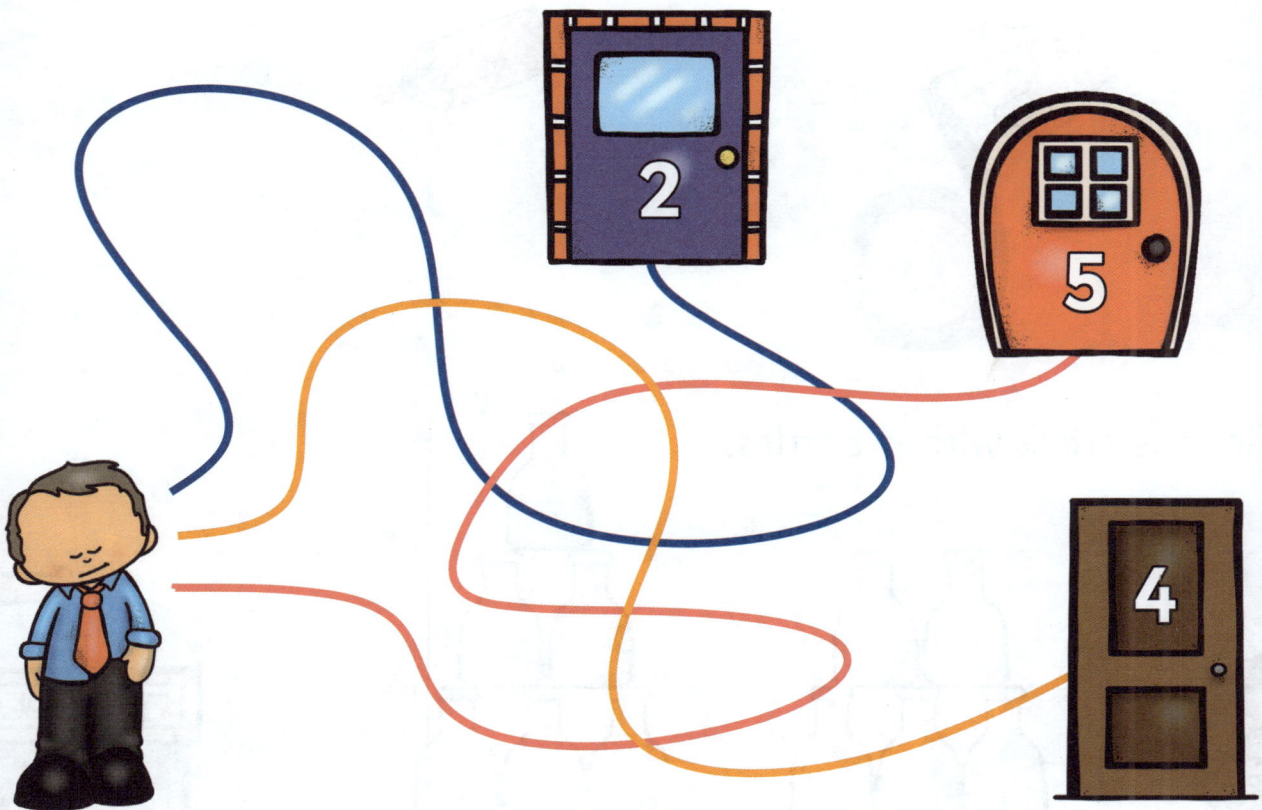

Colour in the smiley face — you're a star with the number 5.

The Number 6

How It Works

Count to 6.

1   2   3   4   5   6

There are 6 ice creams.

Now Try These

Trace the number 6 with your finger.
Then join the dots to write it.

Tick the stack with 6 bottles.

Colour in 6 balloons.

Match each driver to their car.

If you're having fun with number 6, colour in the smiley face!

13

Counting Cards

Look at the picture cards and clues on both pages to solve the puzzles.

Draw lines to match these number cards to the correct picture cards.

1 ball

2 pigs

3 sheep

Find two picture cards that add together to match these number cards.

4	5	6
fish	clouds	birds

How It Works

Count to 7.

1	2	3	4	5	6	7

There are 7 buckets.

Now Try These

Trace the number 7 with your finger.
Then join the dots to write it.

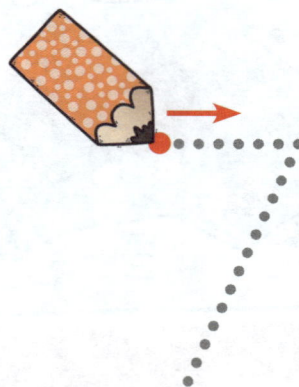

How many people are at the lake? Write the number below.

Circle the bird standing on sign number 7.

1

7

4

6

5

Count the fish. Colour them in.

You've got the number 7 sorted! Colour in the smiley face.

The Number 8

How It Works

Count to 8.

1   2   3   4

5   6   7   8

There are 8 flowers.

Now Try These

Trace the number 8 with your finger.
Then join the dots to write it.

   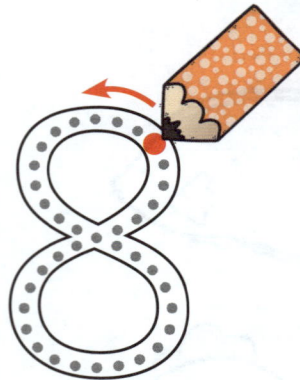

Circle the leaf with 8 ladybirds on it.

Can you find all 8 bugs in the picture below?

How It Works

Count to 9.

| 1 | 2 | 3 | 4 | 5 | 6 | 7 | 8 | 9 |

There are 9 bottles.

Now Try These

Trace the number 9 with your finger.
Then join the dots to write it.

The scientists are bored with their plain white lab coats.
Colour in all 9 coats for them.

Which scientist does clipboard number 9 belong to?

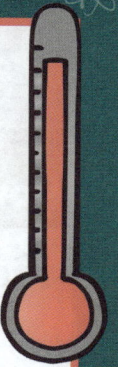

Draw nine books on the bookshelves.

Are you feeling fine with number 9? Colour in the smiley face.

The Number 10

Count to 10.

1	2	3	4	5
6	7	8	9	10

There are 10 kites.

Now Try These

Trace the number 10 with your finger.
Then join the dots to write it.

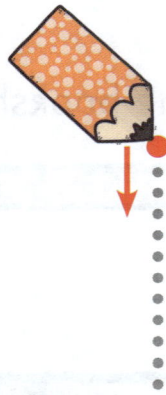

Colour lifeguard number 10 in **red**.
Now colour the others in a different colour.

2   10   5   8

22

How many beach balls are there in the scene below?
Write your answer in the box.

Draw a path from the crab to the rock pool.
Follow the numbers from 1 up to 10 in order.

1	8	5	6	7
2	3	4	2	8
10	7	9	6	9
5	4	3	1	10

Colour in the smiley face if you're feeling 10 out of 10!

How It Works

The monkey has more fruit than the parrot.

The parrot has less fruit than the monkey.

Now Try These

Tick the animal that weighs less.

Circle the animal that has more legs.

Tick the penguin that has less money.

Draw some more stripes on the zebra.

Colour in the smiley face if you know more than you did before!

25

Adding

How It Works

Count the cats to add them together.

   and      makes

2   and   **1**   makes   **3**

Now Try These

Chloe has 1 rabbit and Zack has 1 rabbit.

How many rabbits are there altogether?

There are 3 dogs in the park.   Here comes 1 more!

How many dogs are there altogether?

Colour in 2 more mice. Add them up.

 and  makes

Add up the bones. Draw the answer.

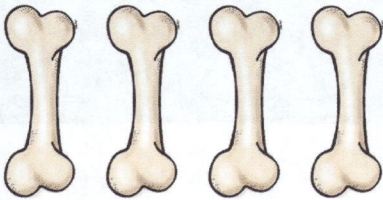 and  makes

4 and 1 makes

Count the hamsters to fill in the boxes.

 and  makes

and makes

Is everything adding up now? Colour in the smiley face.

27

Shapes

How It Works

Some shapes have names.

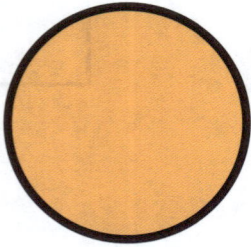

Circle

Square

Triangle

Now Try These

Match all the things that have the same shape.

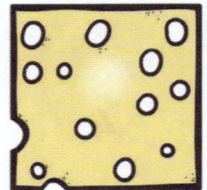

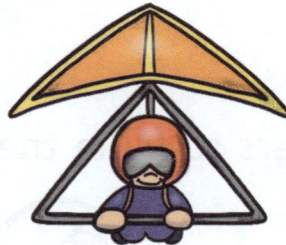

Join the dots to finish the shapes.
Then match each shape with its name.

 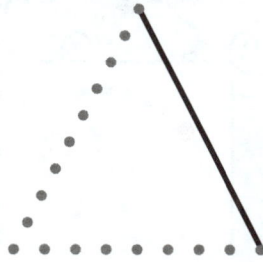 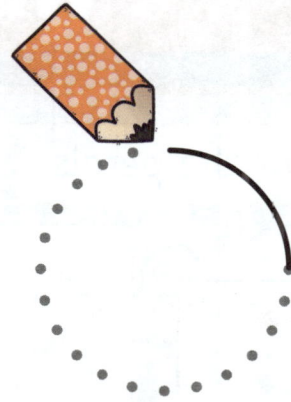

Square   **Circle**   **Triangle**

Colour all the circles in orange.
Colour all the squares in blue.
Colour all the triangles in green.

Are your skills shaping up nicely? Colour in the smiley face.

Writing Numbers

Count the petals.

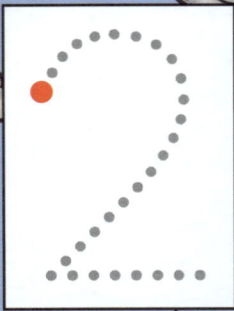

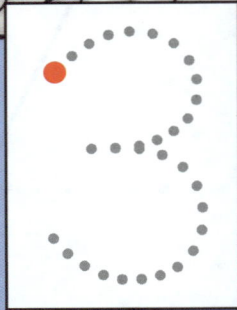

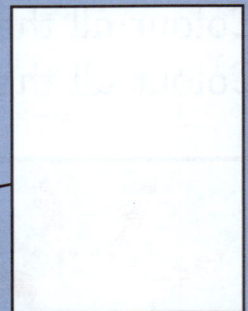

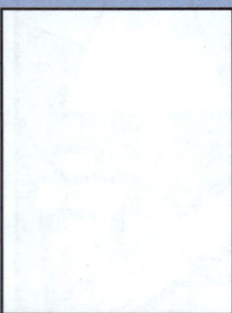

1

2

3

Join the dots to finish the picture.

MPFEQ01